PRESENTED TO

BY

STORIES
of HOPE

from a Bend in the Road

DAVID
JEREMIAH

J. Countryman

Nashville, Tennessee

Published by J. Countryman®, a division of Thomas Nelson, Inc.,
Nashville, Tennessee 37214

Published in association with Yates and Yates, LLP, Literary Agent,
Orange, California.

Project editor: Jenny Baumgartner

Designed by Koechel Peterson and Associates, Inc.
Minneapolis, Minnesota

ISBN 0-8499-5708-7

Printed and bound in the United States of America

www.jcountryman.com

For every pilgrim in this journey of life,

the road will bend in a different direction.

We can never know in advance

which way it will turn,

for the map doesn't display

that kind of detail for us.

We must walk on until we meet the bend

or the dip or the steep, uphill climb

that has been set in the path for each of us.

And we look to God for the grace

to meet that defining moment.

DAVID JEREMIAH
FROM *A BEND IN THE ROAD*

Table of Contents

SECTION THREE: SIGNS OF FAITH

SECTION FOUR: A LIGHTED PATH

Preface

When I first began to share my "bend in the road" experience with cancer, people would come to me and tell me their own personal stories. I discovered that most people have had "disruptive moments" in their lives, or unexpected times of struggle. Through those situations, however, they found a new appreciation for the grace of God.

As I thought about the blessing their personal stories had been to me, I decided to invite the listeners of our radio program, Turning Point, to write about their own "bend in the road" experience and send it to our ministry headquarters. I anticipated that we might receive forty or fifty such stories. To my utter amazement, over eight hundred stories were submitted.

We have chosen twenty-two stories of hope to share with you in this book, including my own. If you are going through a particularly difficult time in your life, then look for comfort in these stories. When you read them, you will find that you are not alone. The Bible says there is no testing that is not common to man (1 Cor. 10:13).

The Bible also reminds us that "God is able" (2 Cor. 9:8). Our disruptive moments give us the opportunity to experience the hand of Almighty God in our lives.

I think you will find His grace in the stories you are about to read. I pray they will encourage your heart and renew your hope.

Dr. David Jeremiah

GRACE

Grace for the Journey

Grace comes into the soul,

      as the morning sun comes into the world;

   first a dawning; then a light;

      and at last the sun in his full

        and excellent brightness.

THOMAS ADAMS

A Moment of Discovery

DR. DAVID JEREMIAH
El Cajon, California

On an ordinary Monday morning in September of 1994, I took a leisurely drive to La Jolla, California, for a routine physical exam. I remember feeling confident about my good health as I progressed through the tests—that is, until the head physician found a mass in my abdomen. A subsequent CAT scan found that the mass was on my spleen, and three radiologists agreed that I had lymphoma, a cancer that attacks the lymphatic system, of which the spleen is the center.

The last word I expected to hear was *cancer*. When the reality hit me, I had to face it.

Almost immediately, I flew to the Mayo Clinic for tests and exploratory surgery, and the doctors officially diagnosed me with non-Hodgkin's lymphoma. In the fall of 1994, I began chemotherapy.

During that time, I found strength in the hundreds of encouraging cards from Turning Point listeners

> *If you are going through*
>
> *a bend in the road,*
>
> *then remember this:*
>
> *Your crisis is important to God.*

and friends and family. I also found great comfort in the Psalms as I identified with the struggles of David.

David wrote many psalms about hurrying into God's presence in fear and trembling. It's certainly one of the great themes of the Psalms. David uses three key metaphors for God: "God, You are my strong refuge . . . You are my rock and my fortress."

I sought the refuge of my Lord. My battle with cancer taught me the importance of a daily dependence on God. My Type A personality had to shift from self-reliance to God-reliance.

Some people have asked me if I was afraid, and the answer is yes. A good bit of my fear focused on the possibility of losing precious years with the people I love. I treasure my family.

Eventually, though, the chemotherapy removed my cancer, and I enjoyed three years of remission.

Then in Thanksgiving of 1998, I traveled to Boone, North Carolina, to attend my youngest son's college football game. I awoke in the middle of the night drenched in sweat. Soon after, doctors confirmed the presence of the lymphoma. Within four months, I underwent a stem cell transplant, an aggressive treatment that involved injecting high doses of toxic chemicals into my body. For five days, I barely existed; I was loaded with morphine to ease the pain as I waited for my white blood cells to rebuild.

As I was recovering from the stem cell transplant, my wife and I stayed in a hotel near the outpatient center of Scripps Clinic. Our spirits were low. I arose early on Easter Sunday morning and made my way to our hotel room's living area. I surfed the television to find something to help lift my mood and found a broadcast from a large church—Easter music, church pageantry, and worship. I sat back, soaked it all in, and lost myself for a few moments. I lowered my guard, and without any clue to what was about to happen, I suddenly began to sob convulsively.

Just then, Donna rounded the corner, her eyes like great ovals. "Are you all right?" she asked.

"No, I'm not," I replied. "I want to be in church. I don't belong here. I belong in church." It was a startling moment of discovery for me—realizing just how deep was my craving to be among the people of God on His day.

For me, it's not about preaching, but the experience of genuine, godly worship in the context of the living, celebrating body of Christ. At that moment, I made a deep, serious vow that I would improve, that I would be among my brothers and sisters again, praising God.

Today, I live in remission. My life can be characterized as the sweet calm after the storm. I suppose the storm passed with the stem cell transplant. On Mother's Day of 1999, I returned to Shadow Mountain Community Church to preach for the first time, and I'm in better physical shape now than ever.

If you are going through a bend in the road, then remember this: Your crisis is important to God. He is using it to make you a more valuable servant to His kingdom. The moment we accept that our crisis has been permitted, even intended by God, our perspective will change. We then find ourselves realizing that God does not allow pain without a purpose . . . and we will hurry into the presence of God for true security and ultimate comfort.

Think of that:

> *strength enshrined in weakness, power in pain.*

It completely defies and undermines

> *the human approach to things—*

> *and that's why it glorifies God.*

"My grace is sufficient for you,

for My strength

is made perfect in weakness."

2 CORINTHIANS 12:9

The weaker we are,

the stronger His grace is revealed.

Or to put it another way:

When "this little light of mine" becomes dimmer,

His great floodlight shines all the more brightly.

DAVID JEREMIAH
FROM *A BEND IN THE ROAD*

Choosing God's Grace

ANN
West Chester, Pennsylvania

God ministered to me in an unbelievable way when I was at a bend in the road in my life. It happened on September 24, 1994, when my nineteen-year-old daughter was killed in a car accident.

After her death, I had to choose between moving on with God's help or allowing myself to be overcome by depression, anger, and bitterness. With deep pain in my heart, I chose to totally lean on the Lord. If He allowed this to happen, then I trusted that He would get me through it. My husband and I both believed that if we looked for God in the situation, we would find Him there. We found His Word to be absolutely true.

Two weeks after the funeral, I returned to my job as a schoolteacher. At the start of every morning, I asked the Lord to give me a clear head and enable me to keep laughing with my students— His Grace was unbelievable! I functioned so well

I have been blessed

as I give others

some of the comfort

that God gave to me.

that year that I was often stopped by teachers and parents who would ask, "How do you do it? How do you keep smiling?" I was able to witness to them by explaining that my strength came from my faith and trust in the Lord Jesus Christ.

Some people probably thought I was in shock or denial, but that wasn't true. Many days, as I drove home, tears rolled down my cheeks. I took time to grieve away from school, but God's grace gave me the strength to carry on.

God also provided me with a Christian support group for bereaved parents. I am now actively involved in reaching out to other bereaved parents by encouraging them and giving them books, tapes, poems, music, or anything that might help them. I have been blessed as I give others some of the comfort that God gave to me.

Psalm 40:2–3 says it well: "He also brought me up out of a horrible pit, out of the miry clay, and set my feet upon a rock, and established my steps. He has put a new song in my mouth—Praise to our God; many will see it and fear, and will trust in the LORD."

Losing my daughter Patty is by far the hardest thing I have ever had to deal with, and I believe my survival came from the Lord. I am so grateful for His grace, and I am so thankful that I know I will see Patty again when God takes me to home to heaven. Patty accepted Christ as her savior when she was just a little girl; what a great source of comfort that has been for my husband and I. ❀

With deep

pain in

my heart,

I chose to

totally

lean on

the Lord.

THE BLISS *of Eternity*

Every glimpse of God is His gift,

to lead us to long more for that most blessed,

ever-longing, ever-satisfied longing of Him,

which will be the bliss of eternity.

EDWARD BOUVERIE PUSEY

I t happens to every one of us—not always with
planes or automobiles or loss of family members
or failed marriages. Somehow, all the same, life
comes crashing down. The loss of one's own child
may well be the most excruciating blow a loving
parent can endure, but you can be certain that
every other tragedy life dispenses offers its own
unique form of suffering.

LIFE
comes crashing down

You're never prepared. That's the essence of pain. Possibly for the first time in life, you wonder whether there's any purpose in going on. For the first time, you seem to lack the strength to even rise from bed and perform the little rituals and have the little conversations that give daily life its color and rhythm. With a heart smashed in ten thousand pieces, you have no clue where to turn.

How wonderful, then, is that moment when you discover you can run into the arms of a Father who loves you and weeps with you. What an incredible moment when you fully comprehend that healing is possible. In Psalm 138:7, David wrote, "Though I walk in the midst of trouble, You will revive me."

DAVID JEREMIAH
FROM *A BEND IN THE ROAD*

Just Like Ruth

PAULA
Dallas, Texas

As I sat in my lawyer's office, listening to the final instructions for our court appearance, all I could do was look intently at my wedding ring. I had not taken it off in hopes that something would change. When we left the office, my husband and I went our different ways. I had thirty days to leave our home, and I had no idea where my two-year-old daughter and I would go or what I would do to support her.

Just six months earlier, I had accepted Christ as my personal Lord and savior. The Lord led me to a church where I met four very strong Christian women who prayed for us constantly. My "spiritual mothers" encouraged me to commit the future to God. I did. In fact, I committed my life and my daughter's life to the Lord as well.

I was left with little resources in hand. I didn't have a job, so I took my wedding ring to a jeweler and several other possessions to a pawnshop. The wedding ring paid the rent, and with the money I received from the other items, I purchased a ring. It was a simple cross, and I placed it on the empty finger of my left hand.

In my Bible reading, I came to the Book of Ruth and read about God's faithfulness. When Ruth purposed in her heart to serve the Lord, she didn't realize that He had placed her into His kingdom and activated His plan for Ruth to be part of the line of the Messiah.

Jesus has redeemed us from an impossible situation.

This same Messiah showed me that when I decided to trust Him, I became a modern-day Ruth. Since that time, He has been working in my life, orchestrating circumstances to draw me closer to Him. The Lord says He is my husband and the father to my child (Ps. 68:5). Within two weeks, the Lord provided a job and childcare through my church.

Each time I now look at that simple little ring, it reminds me that He has taken my daughter and I into His household, just as He did with Ruth. Jesus has redeemed us from an impossible situation.

Things are not always easy, but in our covenant relationship, He has promised that we will not be abandoned nor forsaken (Deut. 31:6b). As my relationship with the Lord deepens, so does my dependency on Him. ✣

WEATH

G od never gives up on you; He never ceases to care about you, and He will not abandon His work on you—of which your trial is a part. I love the poignant words in Isaiah 49:15–16: "Can a woman forget her nursing child, and not have compassion on the son of her womb? Surely they may forget, yet I will not forget you. See I have inscribed you on the palms of My hands; your walls are continually before Me."

The word-picture is a revealing one, isn't it?
Try to suggest a relationship more intimate
than that between a mother and her nursing child.
God wants us to realize that even if that woman
could somehow forget the precious child at her breast,
He would never forget you. He even says,
"Your name is written on the palms of My hands."

Such is God's concern for you. He cannot forget you.
No matter what storm you're weathering, you have never
left God's mind or heart.

DAVID JEREMIAH
FROM *A BEND IN THE ROAD*

A Renewed Spirit

ATWELL
Wilmington, North Carolina

On Wednesday morning, January 16, 1990, at 10:45 a.m., I had just finished checking the pump pressure on a wastewater treatment vessel. I was walking to check another pressure alarm when I was struck in the head by a bail of stainless steel wire that was dropped from sixty-five feet above me. I took two steps and fell like a tree.

My head was ringing, and I could not straighten my neck and head. After working twenty-five years in the chemical industry, this certainly was the most horrible thing to ever happen to me. I managed to get to my knees, and I called for help on the radio I carried.

At the hospital, I was given an MRI. The staff sent me back to work in a neck brace because of my badly sprained neck. They said I was lucky to be alive. The blow should have killed me, but my hard hat had helped soften the blow.

> *I suddenly realized that*
>
> *she was not just my neighbor*
>
> *on the phone, but Jesus Christ,*
>
> *who was telling me*
>
> *He had other plans for me.*

Over the next six months, I went through physical therapy, and I took too many pain pills and muscle relaxers. Nothing could get rid of the neck or back pain, so I decided I didn't want to hurt any longer. In August, I put a .357 pistol in my mouth as I sat in my bedroom. The phone on the nightstand started to ring. It was my next door neighbor, a widow who needed something moved in her garage. She knew I couldn't move it but thought my son might be home.

I suddenly realized that she was not just my neighbor on the phone, but Jesus Christ, who was telling me He had other plans for me. So for the next two years, I participated in small group Bible studies, and I read my daily devotional, *The Upper Room*, regularly. Through *The Upper Room*, God kept putting Matthew 25:36 in front of me: "I was in prison and you visited me." I kept

telling God, "I don't know anyone in prison, and I don't even like people in prison." But He said, "I will introduce you to some."

After I participated in a weekend Christian retreat called "Walk to Emmaus," God spoke to me and said, "I want you to become a prison chaplain for me." I was out of work because of a spinal operation and a neck so damaged they would not operate. God sent me to Central Prison, a maximum-security prison in Raleigh, North Carolina, with the Kairos Prison Ministry. After three trips to Raleigh, God worked through me and several other people to start a Bible study at the prison. It was there that I met a seventy-seven-year-old man who had been working in prison ministry for twenty-one years. Through this friendship, God led me to become a chaplain, and I eventually took over my friend's ministry after he lost his battle with cancer.

We serve an awesome God, and He works in mysterious ways. I now am ordained as a Baptist minister, and I am commissioned as a prison chaplain in North Carolina. ❖

...I decided

I didn't want

to hurt any

longer.

THE PATH *of life*

You will show me the path of life;

In Your presence is fullness of joy;

At Your right hand are pleasures forevermore.

PSALM 16:11

A Second Chance

SHEILA
Ruther Glen, Virginia

God's grace has been described as an undeserved gift. God granted me this gift when He gave me a second chance with my mother.

Growing up, I was the youngest of three children and the only girl. My two brothers were nine and ten years older, and they were both very athletic, the stars of their teams in high school. The only area in which I could compete was with our father; I was the apple of his eye.

Our dad, who only had a third grade education, was self-employed in the logging business. As with most people who own their own business, he was very busy and hardly ever took days off. Not surprisingly, my mom managed all of the parenting responsibilities. Thinking back now, I can see that this situation probably caused many arguments between my parents.

God's grace

has been described

as an undeserved gift.

I don't think that my adolescent years were much different than any one else's, but my mother and I did go head-to-head quite a bit. The problem was, I never realized how much and how many times I hurt her feelings and worried her until after I had moved out.

In February 1985, my grandmother died. At that time, my mother and I were planning my wedding for that May, which would take place on my grandmother's birthday, the same day as Mother's Day. I never really thought about how difficult this must have been for my mother until later.

In September of 1985, I received a call from my brother saying that Mom had been taken to the hospital and they didn't know if she would make it through the night. All I could think about

were the things that I had done to hurt my mother and the words that were left unsaid.

My mother had suffered a major stroke. She did make it through the night, but she was totally paralyzed. We spent the next few months in rehabilitation where she tried to learn to walk and talk again. Eventually she regained her ability to talk and walk, but she permanently lost the use of her right arm. She also walked with a limp.

My mom would never drive or knit or crochet again. She couldn't baby-sit her grandchildren and do the things for them that she liked to do. But the one thing that I really remember is that she never complained.

For many years, I blamed myself for Mom's stroke because of what I had put her through. I didn't tell her how I felt until I was thirty-four years old. I had given my life to Christ, and I wanted to make things right, finally telling her how much she meant to me.

Over the next fourteen years, I tried to make sure that Mom knew how much I loved her and how much I wanted to make up for lost time. She and I became best friends. I will never forget God's grace and mercy when He took my mother in her sleep that night in February of 2000. God gave me a second chance to make things right.

My mother

had suffered

a major

stroke.

I certainly didn't deserve that chance. I wish that my mother hadn't suffered through those trials, but because of my mother's stroke, our family—including my father—realized how important she was to us.

I miss my mother terribly, but I know that God won me over because He knew that Mom wasn't going to be with us much longer. Without God and my church family, I don't know how I could get through my grief of losing her. And my hardest task is yet to come. I have my fourth child on the way. This child will never know what a wonderful person his or her grandmother was, but I also know that God will be there to help me talk about her. . . . and when my mother's words come out of my mouth, I'll know she is listening too. ❧

My mom would never drive or knit or crochet again.

The Bridge to Healing

Tell God all that is in your heart,

    as one unloads one's heart,

        its pleasures and its pains, to a dear friend.

Tell Him your troubles,

    that He may comfort you . . .

        show Him the wounds of your heart,

        that He may heal them.

FRANÇOIS FÉNELON

The Heart of a Child

KIMBERLEE
Friendship, Missouri

I am a single parent of a wonderful five-and-a-half-year-old daughter who loves Jesus very much—so much that she shared her love for Jesus with me when she was only four and a half. I received the Lord two weeks before Easter in 1999 and was baptized on Easter evening at the Advent Christian Church.

In October of 1999, I was diagnosed with breast cancer, and in November of 1999, I had a mastectomy at the age of thirty-eight. During that time, I studied the Bible and attended Bible studies, and I had a very supportive pastor. He made himself available to help with our needs during my struggle.

Second Corinthians 12 tells about Paul's vision and thorn. Like with Paul, the Lord showed me that His grace is sufficient. I live by faith, not by sight. Even as I fought my cancer, I knew I had much to look forward to. All through the entire

> *Like with Paul,*
>
> *the Lord showed me*
>
> *that His grace is sufficient.*
>
> *I live by faith, not by sight.*

process of surgery and chemotherapy, as I went in and out of the hospital, I don't recall even once when was I frightened.

The Lord is so good, so gracious, loving, and kind. He leads me and guides me, and He gives me knowledge and wisdom. When everything seems like it is falling apart, He lifts me, tells me it's okay, and He directs me in the way to go.

Just five months ago, my oncologist told me that my health is restored. Praise the Lord! I have a life ahead of me to be a servant to the Lord who is the King of kings. I thank Him every day because I see life as never before. I see it as an opportunity to reach others in two ways. One is in my role as a single parent who loves the Lord. The second is by sharing how the Lord has shown favor upon me through my illness. I believe that the Lord has wonderful plans for this mother and daughter, and I am so excited. ❧

"God deals with you as sons" (Heb. 12:7).

Can you remember facing a disruptive moment as a child? Perhaps you fell from your bicycle and skinned your knee. What was your first impulse? To call for help, of course. And perhaps when you did that, your mother or father called out, "Stay right where you are— I'm coming to help you!"

That's precisely what God says to us: Stay where you are.
I'll be there with you. When life wounds us and we're in
deep pain, we instinctively cry out to God. And it is then that
we hear Him and feel His presence so clearly. In the midst of
tragic circumstances, we can have the richest fellowship with
Christ afforded to us. That's when our faith becomes fully real,
and we experience the assurance of things we've hoped for.

DAVID JEREMIAH
FROM A BEND IN THE ROAD

A Heart That Sees

PATRICIA
Tucson, Arizona

I was born and raised a Catholic and attended a convent boarding school. After I became an adult, I stopped going to church, probably because I'd had too much "church stuff" in my younger years. I later married a man who had been raised as a Baptist but also stopped attending church when he became an adult.

One day I told my husband that I was searching for some purpose or accomplishment for my life. The next day, he came home with a gift for me. It was a Bible, the King James Version. He said all of the answers were in that book. Even though I had been in a convent and Catholic schools most of my life, I had never read the Bible. At that time, Catholics were told they were not qualified to read and interpret the Bible. The priests were the only ones trained to do so.

When I started reading my Bible, I could not put it down. I then started reading the Catholic Bible, or the New American Bible, because I was told it was different, but I found that the meaning was the same. I also read the New International Version and the *Good News Bible* and found that God's Word was the same in each one.

During this time, I came to know Jesus Christ. My husband accompanied me to a little Baptist church where I dedicated my life to the Lord. I was so happy and excited that I shared my new faith with everyone.

Then came my bend in the road.

One month after I dedicated my life to Jesus Christ, my left eye began to bother me. The next day, I lost vision in that eye. I went to the doctor, but he said I shouldn't worry. I had optic neuritis, a temporary inflammation of the optic nerve that would clear up. But it did not go away, and within a very short time, my right eye started bothering me, too. By this time, I was virtually blind. I could not see anything, but thankfully, I had completed reading the Bible. I remembered that Jesus said in the Bible, "the blind shall see," and I started praying that verse over and over.

Finally, I found an explanation for my blindness. The doctors diagnosed me with multiple sclerosis. The news was devastating. I became depressed, I never

By this time,

I was

virtually

blind.

got up, and I laid on the couch all day. I did not wash my hair or my face. I did not put on makeup. I thought, *What good am I? I cannot see!* I kept praying "the blind shall see" over and over, and I thanked Him for teaching me all about His Bible when I had good eyesight.

My life had come to an abrupt halt, and the only thing I could hold on to was Jesus Christ. I had no idea what was to become of me. I was in the darkness for many months. Gradually, I regained a little bit of eyesight in my left eye, but I was not so lucky with my right eye.

My multiple sclerosis did not limit itself to my eyesight; it continued into my limbs. At first, I had to walk with a cane, but the disease progressed. I now am confined to a wheelchair full-time.

I still talk with my Lord. He has blessed me with a beautiful and intelligent service dog, and I belong to a club where handicapped and disabled people train their own dog. I am very limited in strength, but my service dog is at my side all day. We are a team. She opens handicap doors for me and assists me with all other necessary services.

I feel the Lord is leading me to spread His Word. I believe that people are more receptive to a lady in a wheelchair, holding her Bible, with a beautiful service dog at her side. If nothing else, we bring a smile to people's faces. ❀

I was in

the darkness

for many

months.

The Great Comforter

AMYE
Vicksburg, Mississippi

My bend in the road happened on the morning of September 2, 1998, when my only child accidentally shot himself. He was thirteen years old, and he was my whole life.

I didn't understand why God had done this to me. All I ever wanted to be was a mother, but God had taken this away from me.

I am a Catholic, and my husband and I raised our son A. J. to be a Catholic. We had a strong background in the worship of our Lord, but there were so many loose ends that God had to tie together gently and hand to me. He had to go slow in order for me to see that He is good!

After ten years of marriage, my husband and I had adopted A. J. when he was thirteen months old. He was a very happy and well-balanced child up until his last day on earth, but then God took him home. In the midst of my confusion over the loss of my child, God led me to return to the past so that I could recall all the good things He had done.

On one particular day, I was so lonely for A. J. that I cried all day. I desperately searched for a poem that I had written thanking God for giving me A. J. When I calmed down, God guided me to A. J.'s baby book, and there it was, right beside the poem I had written asking God to grant me a child.

I also found something else in that baby book. In the space where new mothers were asked to write their favorite Bible story, I had written about the story of Hannah (1 Samuel 1 and 2). I could relate to Hannah, who was barren for years before the Lord blessed her with her son Samuel. A. J. was my Samuel. Once again, God was showing me His goodness.

It's still difficult sometimes, but God's gentle grace is walking with me daily. I fill my days with as much of His Word that I can. I see things in the Bible that I never saw before; it is as if God has opened my eyes and is keeping them open for new promises. I also listen to Dr. Jeremiah on the radio. It seems that every time I ask God a question, Dr. Jeremiah gives me an answer in what he is teaching that particular day.

I thank the Lord for being with me and my husband as we walk through this fire. I still don't quite understand, but I do know that God is still good. ❀

All I ever wanted to be was a mother, but God had taken this away from me.

A RIVER *Glorious*

Like a river glorious is God's perfect peace,

Over all victorious in bright increase;

Perfect, yet it floweth fuller every day,

Perfect, yet it groweth deeper all the way.

Stayed upon Jehovah, hearts are fully blest;

Finding, as he promised, perfect peace and rest.

FRANCES RIDLEY HAVERGAL

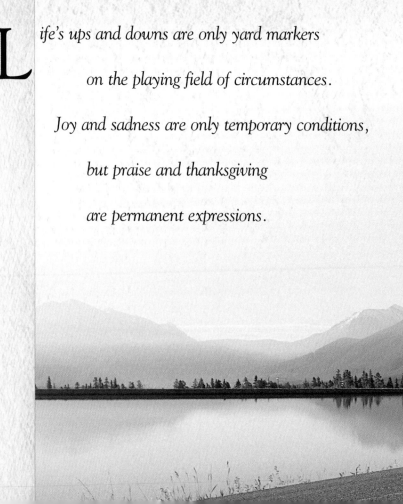

L ife's ups and downs are only yard markers

on the playing field of circumstances.

Joy and sadness are only temporary conditions,

but praise and thanksgiving

are permanent expressions.

When we finally come to understand that truth
and begin to praise God in the midst of all things,
we often find that circumstances themselves change
in our favor. Godly faith changes the world around it,
for we can live triumphantly, knowing that the pain
is temporary and the end has been predetermined;
it's an ending of reunion with the Father and
an eternity in His loving presence.

DAVID JEREMIAH
FROM A BEND IN THE ROAD

For nearly twenty years, I suffered with anorexia. I hid this awful disease for a very long time.

As a child, I was a picky eater. At meals, I often ate a salad with no dressing or tea and toast. From seventh grade through my senior year of high school, I was 5' 7" and weighed 108 pounds. For my height, I should have weighed between 140 and 145 pounds.

When my children were five years and nine months old, my marriage fell apart. My anorexia had become such a problem that I didn't care about anything anymore, and my husband and I divorced.

I eventually met someone new, but that relationship only lasted four and a half years. When the relationship ended, I began to feel even more useless and hopeless than ever. I was devastated on the inside, and the anorexia was damaging my health. I didn't want to live anymore. I planned to commit suicide on June 20, 1996. I was drinking most of that night, and then I went to the garage. I started the car, closed the garage door, and sat there for about forty-five minutes. Then I called on Jesus to help me. I told Him that I couldn't bear the pain any longer. I wanted to overcome my anorexia problem for good. That night, I asked Jesus into my heart.

Finally, after years of struggling with anorexia, I realized that I couldn't do it on my own. At a church service in November of 1997, my pastor called for a prayer chain up at the altar. I went up to a couple I felt the Lord lead me to. For the next five months, I prayed daily. I gave everything I was to God. During one Sunday night service, we sang a song called "I Surrender All," and I lifted up my pain to Him.

In April of 1998, a friend encouraged me to pray for an appetite. I never had an appetite, so I was never hungry. Twenty-four hours after I prayed that prayer, I had an appetite. I felt hungry day after day. On May 10, 1998 (Mother's Day), I gave my testimony that the Lord had healed me of anorexia. I weighed 120 pounds that day; today I weigh 142 pounds.

For anyone suffering from this awful disease, I want tell you that there is hope. Doctor after doctor told me year after year that my organs were going to shut down someday. When I surrendered myself to the Lord, I gave Him control of my life. He is faithful to guide me through the most difficult times. I found that there is nothing too big for the Lord. ❊

I began

to feel even

more useless

and hopeless

than ever.

THE DEEP

G reat works are done in deep waters. If you're diving for pearls, you have to move out of the shallow end. Many of us never learn that lesson; fear restricts us to the comfort zone, where we miss out on untold adventures. But Jesus tells us to launch out into the deep—in risk taking, in the pursuit of excellence, and in the knowledge of Him. We walk to the edge of all our light, and that next step into the blackness holds the destiny God has for us. But it also holds whatever dangers lie in the darkness. We know that, we realize the risks, and perhaps we'll never take that one terrifying step that makes the miracle possible.

THINGS *of God*

No one ever said it would be easy out in the deep waters.
No one ever guaranteed fair weather and smooth sailing.
It's your choice—stay along the shore and you'll always
be safe from drowning and disaster. But you'll also never
know the blessings of the deep things of God.

DAVID JEREMIAH
FROM *A BEND IN THE ROAD*

The Road to Forgiveness

LAJUANA
Chicago, Illinois

I loved my father as long as I could remember. I was daddy's girl. But when I turned twenty-five, I no longer wanted to be daddy's girl. My father did some things in his life that I found unforgivable at that time. I had placed my father high on a pedestal, and he had fallen. Because I could not forgive my father, I was terribly disturbed. I could not rest, and I was deeply depressed. My doctor prescribed an anti-depressant, but it did not seem to be the answer for me.

For two years, a male friend had pursued me for a date. He wanted to be more than friends, but I just wanted a friend. I had lost my best friend—my father—and I was looking for a friend that I could count on. I did not want to invest my heart in another person who would break it. I did not want to put another person on a pedestal only to be disappointed again.

My heart was freed by the

passage in Matthew 6:12,

"Forgive us our debts,

as we also have forgiven

our debtors."

One day, when I felt overwhelmed by my sadness with my father, I went to visit my friend. I did not know where else to turn. I could no longer function. In response, my friend pulled me toward him. At first, I thought that he was trying to take advantage of the situation, but then he said, "Come pray with me." He helped me to my knees, and we prayed a simple prayer, the Lord's Prayer.

My heart was freed by the passage in Matthew 6:12, "Forgive us our debts, as we also have forgiven our debtors." I had said that prayer a million times, but on that day, it took on a new meaning. I was able to forgive my father, and I began to forgive myself for idolizing him rather than just loving him.

Then by the grace of God, I received an unexpected surprise. I began to see my friend in a

new light. I saw his efforts to walk as a Christian, and I married him two years later. We have been married for six years, and even though the doctors said that I would never have children, we have been blessed with two children.

Just six months into our marriage, I was diagnosed with cancer, but by God's power, I'm still here. My husband loved me through chemotherapy, baldness, and radiation therapy. And standing next to my husband throughout that ordeal was my father, my friend.

I thank the Lord that unworthy as I am, I am truly blessed to have a father and a husband, and in them, two special friends. ❁

I could not

rest, and

I was deeply

depressed.

HE BESTOWS *on us*

I pray God may open your eyes

and let you see what hidden treasures

he bestows on us in the trials

from which the world thinks only to flee.

JOHN OF AVILA

I will lift up my eyes to the hills—

From whence comes my help?

My help comes from the Lord,

Who made heaven and earth.

He will not allow your foot to be moved;

He who keeps you will not slumber.

PSALM 121:1–3

NTAINTOP

Despite the perils we encounter,

     the mountainous crags and the desert wastelands,

     we can trust the Lord.

Yes, He is awesome and we feel small

       and insignificant,

     but the psalmist assures us that God

       bridges the gap.

He is never too great to care;

     we are never too small for His caring.

DAVID JEREMIAH
FROM A BEND IN THE ROAD

A Blessing in Disguise

SARAH
Pt. Richmond, California

"Will it ever go away?" I asked the doctor through tears. The date was August 18, 1994. I had turned eight years old that July, and now it seemed as if life was over. The doctor had just diagnosed me with juvenile diabetes.

Since I was only eight, I didn't really understand the diagnosis, but when I found out that I would have to prick my fingers to test my blood sugar and take shots (I absolutely hate shots!) for the rest of my life, I was devastated.

When I asked the doctor if it would ever go away, he kind of hung his head and wouldn't look into my eyes. He then responded, "No, Sarah, it will never go away." I turned to my mother's shoulder and cried.

The nurse came in and tested my blood sugar and then gave me a shot. My mom called my dad at work, and he came to the doctor's office.

When I was diagnosed,

I thought, God, WHY? Why me?

Why'd you have to pick me? *But*

now I think, Thank you, God!

I didn't know it at the time, but God had really blessed me. Because we caught my symptoms so early, I didn't get extremely sick. I have a friend who was diagnosed when her blood sugar was over one thousand. Mine was only a little over four hundred. When first diagnosed, some people have to stay in the hospital for a few weeks; I didn't even have to stay for one day.

When I was diagnosed, I thought, *God, WHY? Why me? Why'd you have to pick me?* But now I think, *Thank you, God!* Yes, you read that correctly. My diabetes has been a blessing. It has brought my mom, Lourdes; my dad, John; and my identical twin sister, Vanessa; and I closer together. And it has brought new friends into our lives. It also has been a witnessing tool.

I've had diabetes now for six years. Every year on August 18, my family and I go to an ice-cream shop to celebrate my "anniversary."

I am thirteen now. I still go through occasional times of questioning when I ask, "Lord, Why me?" But if I had to choose any disease in the world, I would choose diabetes. It is hard to deal with sometimes, but at least I can take care of it and live a normal life.

I may have thought life was over when I was eight, but now I know that it was just another step. God can take anything and turn it into something good. ❋

God can take

anything and

turn it into

something

good.

THERE IS *nothing*

There is nothing, no circumstance, no trouble,

no testing that can ever touch me until, first of all,

it has come past God and past Christ, right through to me.

If it has come that far, it has come with great purpose.

ALAN REDPATH

Signs of Faith

Faith is the belief that God is real and that God is good.

Faith is not a mystical experience or a midnight vision or a

voice in the forest . . . it is a choice to believe that the one

who made it all hasn't left it all and that he still sends light

into shadows and responds to gestures of faith.

MAX LUCADO

A Gift from the Lord

MARY
San Antonio, Texas

When I was young, I thought I'd marry a knight in shining armor and live happily ever after. But that dream had to meet reality.

I accepted the Lord Jesus Christ as my savior at the age of eleven. Even at that early age, I yearned for something to fill the emptiness in my life, and Jesus filled the emptiness. After accepting the Lord, I got involved in my local Baptist church. I did everything you could imagine—from being president of my youth group and Sunday school secretary to teaching vacation Bible school. I was even the church pianist at age twelve. I felt that God had something special in store for me.

As I was growing up, I knew that I was going to marry a preacher. At the age of seventeen, when my parents let me date—in groups, that is—I dated only Christian young men, most of whom were studying for the ministry. I never had a desire to date anyone that did not know Jesus as his savior.

At the age of twenty-one, I met the man who would be my husband. He was studying at a Bible school, preparing for the ministry. We dated and became engaged, and after one year, we married. It seemed to be a marriage made in heaven. Two years later, we had our first child, a little girl. Two years after her birth, I miscarried our son. I didn't think that there could be a more difficult experience in my life than losing a baby. Later, we had two more children, a son and another daughter.

I was happy, though being a pastor's wife had its difficult times. I felt that I lived in a glass house, always conscious about my life and my children, always feeling that everything needed to be perfect because that was what everyone expected. I survived the pressure, but my husband couldn't. He told me that he felt trapped and unhappy. He then said that at a revival meeting where he was preaching, he had met a woman, and they "fell in love." My husband left our family, divorced me, and married the other woman.

I survived

the pressure,

but my

husband

couldn't.

The pain that I felt was unbearable. It was devastating to know that someone else had the man that I thought was mine. I didn't desire to live. The only thing that kept me going were my children and my faith in God. Christian friends assured me that something good would come out of the bad. God's love and mercy kept me sane. I knew that He wouldn't give me more than I could bear.

I enrolled in school and started taking night classes

to finish my degree. I also began working full-time. With three children in school, needless to say, I sometimes wondered if I would make it. My car was always broken, and I had to find rides to work and school. Family members would pick up my children from school. I thank God for the "yellow banana" (the school bus), as my children knew it.

For five years, my children and I stuck it out and cried and prayed together. We attended numerous Christian activities, such as Bible studies and concerts, to fill our lives with God's Word and comfort.

Then one day, I met my soon-to-be husband, Manuel, who had lost his first wife to cancer. He had five children. Two were young and still lived with him, and three were married.

He invited me for coffee, and we left my three children and his two with my older daughter. We had a good time on our date, but not surprisingly, both sets of children were hesitant to share their only parent. When we went out after that, we often included the children in our activities. Boy, did we have our share of ice cream and movies!

Manuel and I soon discovered that we were falling in love. I was scared and wondered if we could survive this. I struggled and even sent Manuel away many times. I told him that I was not going to marry another preacher, especially one with children.

But love won me over. We married, and Manuel continued to pastor. It wasn't always easy for our blended family to come together. There were struggles, but our love kept us together and made us stronger. Eventually, Manuel took a year off to train full-time to become a hospital chaplain. He then served as a chaplain for several years in a hospital setting, ministering to hurting people.

Manuel showed me what love was all about. He loved me unconditionally, and he loved others unconditionally. I never heard a harsh word come out of his mouth. I knew that he was my blessing and my reward for persevering in the midst of my painful circumstances for so many years.

One month short of our tenth anniversary, Manuel was admitted to the hospital. As he laid in the hospital bed, I knew that the Lord was going to take him. I knew that my angel, my reward, was going home. Without my confidence in God, I think I would've gone crazy. When I look around at the pictures of my beloved, Manuel, I realize the blessing that was given to me, and I thank God for the wonderful memories. ❁

BUILD

The same God who has been there for you in the past

is the God who is going to be there for you

in the future.

He will bring resolution in His own time,

according to His own purposes.

We become preoccupied with our circumstances;

God is preoccupied with our character.

He will allow the tough times for the higher good of our character

until He is finished with the great work

that is invisible to our earthly eyes.

DAVID JEREMIAH
FROM *A BEND IN THE ROAD*

A Greater Perspective

GERALD
Grabill, Indiana

One foggy evening on October 12, 1984, my wife and I were attending a football game at our local high school. Our younger son, Mike, was out with friends, and our teenage daughters, Ann and Cindy, were spending the evening at home. Our eldest son, Scott, was away in the Air Force, stationed in Grand Forks, North Dakota.

At the game, the home team was losing, and I noticed that my wife was not enjoying being there for some reason—a reason she did not understand herself. She felt restless, and it rubbed off on me. We noticed that the EMS vehicle had to leave the playing field just before halftime, but we didn't think much about it. My wife, Pat, finally told me that she wanted to wait in the car. In the car, she prayed, asking the Lord to show her what was wrong, but no answer came. I decided to leave the game a few minutes later.

We arrived home, but the house was empty. Immediately, we looked for a note from the girls but couldn't find one, which was out of character for them. In our close family, we always kept each other informed of our whereabouts. My wife and I assumed that they had gone to a friend's house and would be calling us at any moment. They wouldn't have expected us to arrive home early.

We turned on the television to the World Series game and waited. As time passed, we became more anxious. Mike had returned home early and was already in bed, but he got up when he heard us. He mentioned that he heard someone had been hit and killed by a train in Grabill.

This increased our anxiety, so we began to call friends to see if anyone knew about the accident. My wife even drove over to Grabill to see if she could learn anything. No one would (or could) tell her who was involved. While she was gone, a friend said that the accident had just been shown on the 10 p.m. news, and the car was gold and white—the same as OUR CAR! We knew in our hearts then that we had lost our girls.

About thirty minutes later, we saw a beam from a spotlight shining on our mailbox. Pat and I held each other and prayed for strength. As the sheriff's deputy and the department chaplain entered our home, the Lord gave us such a peace in our hearts—

We knew in our hearts then that we had lost our girls.

words cannot express it. Our fears were confirmed officially. Both girls had died instantly.

But had we **lost** our girls? Each one had chosen to put their faith and trust in Jesus Christ as their personal savior. So the very moment that their life ended on this earth, they were ushered into the presence of the Lord.

Years earlier, our entire family had come to the Lord by His grace. When Pat and I were planning to be married, we had to be baptized so that we could join the church before the wedding. Jesus Christ had very little to do with our decision. We then married and lived fairly normal lives.

Our first child was born in 1961, and Pat began to feel that something was lacking in her life. As Scott grew, her emptiness grew also. She began to take Scott to church, trying to fill this void. Then, one evening in September of 1963, she was watching Billy Graham on television. After the broadcast, she bowed her head and asked Jesus to come into her heart and take over her life. From that moment, her life was changed. She developed an avid interest in the Bible and God's plan for her life. She and Scott continued to go to Sunday school and church.

Gradually, I began to attend. Then, in November of 1964, an evangelist came to our church for a week of services. I felt a strong need to attend the meetings. I went every evening and heard what it meant to become a Christian, but I could not bring myself to go down the aisle to give my life to Christ. On Thursday of that week, we invited the evangelist and the pastor and their wives to our home for cake and coffee. As we talked around the table, the conversation came around to me. I admitted that I was not a Christian. I bowed my head right there and asked the Lord to forgive me of my sins and to come into my heart. And just like that, He did!

From that moment on, my outlook on life changed. I also received a peace in my heart that I had never known before. I began to live for the Lord instead for myself. Our children did not wait as many years as we did. Each one became a Christian at an early age.

It was the power of God that drew Pat and I to Him, and it was that same power that brought us through the loss of our daughters. Without Him, we would have fallen apart.

Through this tragedy, we became keenly aware of the importance of putting people first. We had already been concerned about the salvation of others, but our experience prompted us to start a small personal ministry in which we become pen pals to prisoners and anyone else who is interested. Through God's leading, we've also become an associate school for Source of Light Ministries International.

God is so wonderful! ❧

GIVING

I n the storm or in the earthquake or in the midst of any
disaster threatening to engulf us—that's the time
we feel the presence of the Lord as we've never felt
Him before. Other so-called friends may disappear.
Their words may falter and their support may vanish.
But God is close in crises, surrounding us with
His presence. He promised us He would do it,
and our Lord is always as good as His word.

David, recipient of the honorary degree in Crises and Catastrophes, bears testimony to that fact. His acceptance speech for such a degree would sound much like one of the psalms: thanks and praise to God Almighty, who keeps His promises. But at the end of the speech, David would add one more startling idea. He would assure you that the Lord will not only protect you, but He will perfect you.

DAVID JEREMIAH
FROM *A BEND IN THE ROAD*

Lightning and Thunder

KRISTIN
Cleveland, Ohio

"Lord, I need a change in my life, one that will keep me away from the misguided life I am leading now." I prayed this simple prayer at the beginning of my junior year at Ohio University. It's one I am sure many have prayed, but I didn't stop there. I continued, "And when this change happens, make it strike like lightning."

I didn't know the mighty, all-powerful God very well when I sincerely lifted up that prayer. But I got to know Him well and quickly when I saw the lightning and felt the thunder of my answered prayer. The answer was delivered in a green-walled nurse's station at the university clinic when a nurse informed me that I was pregnant.

The news was a shock. I was raised in a wonderful Christian home. Being the oldest of six children, I felt like a guinea pig many times in my parents' child-raising dilemmas, but they were great parents, always striving to raise us to be good, godly men and women of God. As for me, I was the average "good kid" through grade school and high school. I wanted to rebel and be wild, but I was too shy and too afraid of what my parents and family would say. When I got to college, however, I loved the freedom. I was on my own to make choices, with no one around to remind me of the moral code I should have been living by.

I lived the carefree life for two years. I was drinking and partying—the late nights, the boys. I was having fun . . . so I thought. But as time went on, I felt more and more empty. At the beginning of my junior year, my boyfriend and I broke up, and I was adjusting to new roommates. These two events opened my eyes to the shallow relationships I then had with the people in my "party scene."

I was having

fun . . .

so I thought.

I longed for the true, most meaningful relationship one could ever have—a relationship with Jesus Christ. I then prayed for a change that would "strike like lightning" so that I could begin a new life with my Lord and savior.

The Lord answered me in an amazing way. One night at party, I met a guy who asked me to go next door with him to see his pet chameleon. I should have run in the other direction, but I decided to go. My intentions were to keep things from going too far, but I don't remember much after I followed him to his apartment.

Four months later, I found out that I was pregnant. Because of my rapid memory loss, it has been speculated that he put a drug in my drink.

After I received the news, I began a long, painful journey with God. He guided me through mending myself and rebuilding my relationship with Him, my family, and my friends.

That event changed my life completely. I never thought God would answer my prayer in such a way. It made me see how much God loves me and how He will stop at nothing, such as letting me suffer the consequences of sin, in order to get my attention.

Today, I have a wonderful three-year-old son named Joshua Samuel. Joshua means, "Jesus is salvation," and Samuel means "God's gift." It was a hard road to take, but I now have a precious gift that I don't deserve. God showered me with abundant grace. The son he gave to me is my daily inspiration to seek the ultimate gift, the Son that God wants us all to receive. ❦

Four months

later, I found

out that I was

pregnant.

A Repentant Heart

JOHNNY
Hutchinson, Kansas

Recently, the bottom fell out of my life. I was at the top of my career in the military and in church, but my marriage was falling apart. The oncoming divorce coupled with the tremendous stress of my job and church was too much. I tried to run away from everything.

Shortly after I made the decision to turn my back on everything that mattered in my life, I foolishly committed a crime that stood to wipe out everything I cared about. In those first few days of legal dealings, I felt compelled to end my life. The shame and the hopelessness of what my family and I would have to bear was overwhelming.

From the moment I was charged with my crime, my wife told me she would stand by me and would not divorce me. I prayed to God for strength and found myself in tears each day for about three weeks. I just couldn't see how my family would survive without me. Just when it seemed that I couldn't go on anymore, I felt a warmth in my heart that I had never felt before. It was a peaceful feeling. It was strange that my situation had not changed, yet I felt this peace.

I know now that it was God's grace. He had heard my prayers, despite the great sin I had committed. Each day after that, I began to grow again in God. I read my Bible earnestly and found that it was like reading the Word for the first time. Slowly, God began to show me how my family and I would survive. He repaired the painful division between my wife and I.

He also showed me that we had people around us who would stand by us, no matter what. What seemed impossible at the beginning now seemed possible, even against great odds. My wife and I both went through a transformation that could only have come from God.

Today, I sit in prison, and I will be here for four years. But I have a peace within myself that I have never had. For I feel closer to God than I have ever felt in my life. God has taken care of my family, and I know He will forever.

As I look back now, I know I have not earned God's peace or blessings. It only by God's grace that my wife and I are in love and still have our family and our home. Our relationship with God is closer than ever, and it has become the center of our lives. I will serve Him because I love Him. He has given His grace because He loves us. ❊

I just couldn't

see how my

family would

survive

without me.

I may not know you by name,
  but I'm certain that if you're not treading
  through the dust of despair at this very moment,
  the time is certain to come.
But when that day arrives, you will not face it unarmed.
The Bible, sharper than any two-edged sword,
  stands ready for combat.
It contains desert psalms that can become your battle plans.
The ammunition of praise is ready for discharge.
And close by your side will be a faithful, powerful God
  filled with lovingkindness and plans for you,
plans that lead to spiritual victory and personal fulfillment.

DAVID JEREMIAH
FROM *A BEND IN THE ROAD*

On a Wednesday night, my husband and I returned home after a worship service and answered the phone. The voice on the other end said, "Joyce, your son is dead. He has taken his life in an extremely tragic way." I remember saying, "No, not my son. There has got to be some mistake. This can't be happening to me. This only happens to someone else."

But it was true. I remember feeling like the life was draining out of my soul, and this thought came to my mind: *Lord, I don't understand.*

Only a month before, I had been praying for him so desperately. I knew he was having some problems, and I knew God was His only answer. So I said, "Lord, I don't know what else to do but to turn him over to you." I prayed, and I released him to the Lord.

I thank my God

for loving me so much

and for the blessings

I have everyday.

I didn't understand why this had happened, but I got down on my knees and asked my heavenly Father to help me. "I can't get through this without you," I said. Then God brought these words to my heart: "My love for my God is greater than the grief I bear." And I thanked the Lord for letting me have my son for thirty-three years.

My son had two little boys, ages two and five. They had barely gotten to know their father. I prayed for them, and although I continued in my faith for my God, I still prayed, "Please God help me to understand this!"

One morning, I awoke and felt like someone had poured cold water on me. First Corinthians 13 was stuck in my mind. I picked up my Bible and started reading, and then I was really confused.

The Scripture was about love. I asked my husband, "What is God trying to say to me?" I read it over and over, but I could not understand. I asked God to reveal it to me somehow.

I listen to Turning Point every day and enjoy the teachings of Dr. Jeremiah. As I was listening one morning, I will never forget hearing Dr. Jeremiah ask his listeners to tune in the next week because he would be starting a new series on 1 Corinthians 13. He would be speaking about the love of God, and needless to say, I did listen.

Now I do understand what God was trying to say to me. He wanted to tell me how much He loves me. Although I will never understand why my son died, God has given me a peace in my heart and a chance to witness of His wonderful love. He is the God of all comfort, and I now understand what others are going through when they lose a child.

I thank my God for loving me so much and for the blessings I have everyday. Because of this terrible crisis in my life, I pray that I can be a comfort to others for His honor and glory. ❈

"I can't get

through this

without you,"

I said.

Trusting the Character of God

JUDY
Quarryville, Pennsylvania

"God is good all the time, and all the time God is good," George said to me as he reached to shake my hand. The church service was good as usual, I suppose, but I hadn't been able to enter into worship nor could I remember one word of the sermon. Grief consumed so much of my being that I mostly felt numb.

Just a few weeks earlier, following our church's Easter celebration, my brother had died unexpectedly at the age of forty-three. Despite a visit to the hospital ER and an EKG at the doctor's office, professionals were unable to detect a heart attack in progress.

Bob was more than just a brother. We grew up in a violent home. Without warning, Dad would go into violent rages that usually ended with him beating my mother. Growing up, we held on to the hope that someday we'd be old enough to leave home. No longer would Dad have control over us. As children, Bob and I would daydream about what our lives would be like as adults. He wanted to run his own business, own horses, and collect classic cars. I wanted marriage and children.

Finally, we grew up and left home. Numerous times in my life, Bob stood in the gap for Dad. He attended my high school and nursing school graduations. My dream of marriage came true in 1976, and Bob was my escort down the aisle. Dad did not attend any of our graduations or either of our weddings.

Bob was

more than

just

a brother.

Years later, when we were both married and had children, Bob telephoned my home one December and posed as the voice of Santa Claus, asking my children what they wanted for Christmas.

Bob operated his own automobile body repair shop. Often he was his own worst enemy by showing too much compassion to his clients in allowing them to take their cars before they paid their bill. Bob liked to act tough, but he had a gigantic, soft heart behind the face of coarse whiskers. Black T-shirts and collar-length hair gave him the appearance of a rough character, but laughter and compassion softened his countenance.

Kim, Bob's wife, and I had been friends since we were young teenagers. We had supported each other through many difficult situations. She and Bob stood by me when our mobile home burned to the ground on New Year's Day in 1997. A few years later, Bob lost his body shop garage to a fire. Many friends gathered in support to rebuild the structure.

Early in the morning of April 11, 1996, the telephone startled me from sleep. It was Kim, frantic and tearful as she proceeded to tell me that the ambulance was at her house, that the EMT workers told her that they believed that Bob was suffering a heart attack. Within fifteen minutes, I arrived at their house. I saw Kim and the children huddled together in the living room. The EMT workers were administering CPR, and Bob laid on the floor in unprecedented helplessness.

Emotionally

I had never

felt so alone.

"How's he doing?" I chokingly asked.

"It's not good," a man answered.

A Christian for many years, I had served as Sunday school teacher and women's ministries director. I had even founded a ministry outreach and spoke at numerous churches, but now I needed to dig deep for the faith that I needed.

The EMTs lifted the stretcher over the bed toward the doorway. By now chest percussions were only intermittently administered. As they passed by me, I reached out and took hold of Bob's warm wrist, partly to feel for a pulse, and partly to speak in prayer.

"In the name of Jesus," I said as tears began streaming down my cheek. I'm not sure if the words were said in hopes of resurrecting Bob, or spoken as a way of acknowledging that my brother had passed on to death.

Emotionally I had never felt so alone. My husband, Ted, offered a shoulder and an ear whenever necessary, but it felt as though I couldn't convey the extremely deep pain that I was feeling. It was like none that I had ever experienced.

Weeks had passed and I went to church every Sunday. Normally, I could enter into the contemporary worship with ease. Joyfully, I would sing praises to God despite whatever turmoil was happening in my life. But this time it was different. I had to struggle just to do simple, normal, everyday things, much less sing out or raise my hands in praise. Sometimes I'd try hard to make a sound as I attempted to sing, but my throat felt swollen and the feeble attempt gave way to tears.

On that special Sunday, the service ended, and I wanted to go home. Ted was talking with a few people, and I stood off to the side in an attempt to avoid conversation. I would be able to maintain what little composure I had as long as I didn't have to talk to anyone.

George was a steadfast man of God. He was bold in his speech and actions. Not really knowing him personally, I had felt that George was one of those people that had lost touch with reality and operated on a level of spirituality that was untouchable by "normal" people.

Hiding in my world of grief and longing to go home, I didn't notice George coming up behind me.

"Hey, little one," he stated.

I turned, knowing by the voice that it was George. I couldn't speak. All I could do was give a feeble smile.

"God is good all the time," said George.

Not wanting to verbally disagree with him and overwhelmed by grief, I just stood there motionless. "God is good all the time," he repeated as he extended his hand to mine.

Expressionless, I stared past his shoulder. I didn't want to make eye contact. I loved God, but with the depth of pain that I was feeling, I couldn't agree that all the time God is good, so I thought it better to not say anything.

"Look at me little one," requested this man in his late fifties.

Emotions welled up inside of me. I turned to look to George with the intention of excusing myself, but I felt stunned as our eyes met. I stared into George's eyes. They shone with such brilliance and depth that I knew it was God's way of communicating with me. Instantly I felt compassion and peace radiate from his eyes to my spirit, and assuredly, I knew that Bob was with Jesus. Inaudibly, I heard the voice of God telling me that Bob was with Him in heaven, and that as painful as it was for me to go through the grief, someday we would be joyfully reunited.

"God is good all the time, and all the time God is good," restated George.

Subtly smiling and with a gentle nod, I acknowledged and agreed with the statement. George softly hugged me, and I walked away for the first time with an inner peace and a sense that somehow things would be all right.

God knew the pain and corruption of this world, so He offered His salvation. It's His promise of better times without hurt, grief, or death. Jesus suffered so that we could have ultimate joy! ❁

Jesus

suffered

so that we

could have

ultimate joy!

WITH THEE *there is light*

In me there is darkness, but with Thee there is light.

I am lonely but Thou leavest me not.

I am feeble in heart, but Thou leavest me not.

I am restless, but with Thee there is patience;

Thy ways are past understanding,

but Thou knowest the way for me.

DIETRICH BONHOEFFER

PATH

A Lighted Path

When the dark clouds gather most, the light is the more brightly revealed to us. When the night lowers and the tempest is coming on, the Heavenly Captain is always closest to His crew.

CHARLES SPURGEON

My story is not one of a dramatic conversion, but rather a story of God's continuing faithfulness in the lives of one of His children.

I had the privilege of being raised in a Christian home. Not only were my parents Christians, but I had a wonderful heritage of faith through godly grandparents and great-grandparents.

In 1980, I graduated from high school, and one year later, I married a man who loved the Lord. My husband worked for his family's prospering business. We were able to buy a little home, and life was good. It was easy to be a Christian. Over four-and-a-half years, we were blessed with three children who were healthy and enjoying life.

Then in 1990, God allowed my world to be rocked. My mom, who was forty-eight at the time, was diagnosed with breast cancer. This news devastated me and my brothers and sisters. I began to question God's timing. My little sister was only ten years old, and I had three small children who needed their grandmother. I remember nights of crying myself to sleep, begging and pleading with God for her healing. Within months, the cancer spread to her bones and ultimately to her brain. Twenty-three months after the original diagnosis, Mom left this world to be with the Lord.

Within a year after losing my mom, our business began to experience some difficult times. Due to poor managerial decisions, the company was in deep financial trouble. We realized that it had to be sold. In order to make up for some of the money that was owed, the lawyer informed us that our house was going to be auctioned off. I couldn't understand how God could allow this to happen.

During this turmoil in our lives, a friend offered us a week's stay at a condo in Florida. On our way back home, we traveled through the mountains. I was nervous about coming home because I didn't know what the future held.

As I drove through the mountains, the sun went down. Soon the sky was dark, and seeing became very difficult. I was afraid, once again feeling like I wasn't in control. God began to speak very clearly to me. I saw little reflectors every one hundred yards or so on the road. Although it was dark outside, those reflectors showed me the way. Whenever there was a curve in the road and I began to get apprehensive, another little square reflector appeared. Through these simple road reflectors, I learned a lesson about God. Through the "mountains," I don't have to see so far ahead of me. I just have to trust that He will provide little markers to show me the way to go.

Looking back, I can see that He placed people in my life that helped me through those difficult times. We did not lose our home, and our family is healing from the loss of a wonderful mom and grandmother. I still have "mountain" experiences in my life that I don't understand, but I am learning to trust God.

Mine is a testimony to God's faithfulness. Even when you can't see Him, He's there and will never leave you. I try to remember that when I am unsure of what the future holds, I know who holds the future. ✤

Mine is

a testimony

to God's

faithfulness.

MY SPIRITUAL *retreat*

You were with me in it all!
    I sense Your vital presence—
Your sure and steady guidance.
    Not once did you leave me stranded.
Perhaps, in Your great wisdom
    You longed to teach me a practical truth:
When You are my Spiritual Retreat
    I need not be a spiritual recluse.

RUTH HARMS CALKIN

I f you've opted to pursue the adventure of following Jesus, you've already discovered that the journey doesn't occur in a luxury limousine. He will lead you to and through some rough places.

It may be that you've found yourself in the "old gospel ship," rocked by the waves and thrashed by the downpour as lightning and thunder boomed all around you.

Tempest

The moment may come when you say, "I didn't sign up
for this! I know I sang, 'Wherever He leads, I'll go,'
but can't we at least check the weather report first? How
could He lead me into a storm like this one?"

Just cling to the knowledge that you could be in no
safer place than a storm of His making. You are safer and
more secure in the tempest with Jesus than you could ever
be in the calmest place without Him. That calm, you'll
come to realize, is an illusion; and the storm is for a good
purpose and a short duration.

DAVID JEREMIAH
FROM *A BEND IN THE ROAD*

Freedom to Believe

CLIFF
Rocky Mount, North Carolina

It was in 1989 when I received a call from the police department; the officer was looking for my wife. I told them that Ann was at home sick, but they had been to the house. No one answered the door.

I quickly went home to check on her. When I walked into the house, I called out her name, and there was no answer. Entering the bedroom, I found her lying across the bed with her wrists slashed. After stopping the bleeding, I questioned her about the police.

Because of a house fire that almost took everything we had, Ann began taking money from her job. She hid the money under the pretense that various churches donated it to us in an attempt to help our desperate situation.

During this time in our life, I was an alcoholic. I drank heavy to moderate amounts, depending on

During this time

in our life,

I was an alcoholic.

how well I was able to cope with problems. Alcohol became my crutch when I couldn't handle things. On that day, my wife was in trouble, but instead of being there for her, I took a bottle, walked out on the front porch, and proceeded to get drunk, leaving my wife to cry herself to sleep.

Then on June 27, I asked Jesus into my life. The Spirit of God hit me so hard I was knocked off my feet to my knees. It was like a vision. I saw the hand of God enter through the top of my head and grab hold of the darkness inside and pull it out. As the sin was coming out of me, the flames of the Holy Spirit were cauterizing my wounds and healing me from within.

A week earlier, Ann had asked me what was I going to do when she went to prison. Was I going to take our children back to Texas? Was

I going to file for a divorce? I asked her if she wanted an honest answer. She said yes. I answered, "I don't know."

After I accepted Jesus into my life, I was able to go back to her and give her an answer. I said that I would wait for her with the help of Jesus.

As the time drew closer to turn Ann over to the federal marshals, I realized that I had another serious problem to deal with—my drinking. At 2 a.m. one morning, tears were running down my face, and I cried out to God to take the alcohol from me.

I heard the Lord speak to my spirit, telling me to pour out the alcohol I had purchased earlier that day. I rose from my bed and poured it out. Then I heard Him tell me to go to bed; He would see me in church the next day. There was a presence of God so strong around me that every inch of my body tingled with joy. I have gone now ten years without a drink.

Ann did go to prison and served three years out of eighteen. With the help of our Lord Jesus, we stayed together. Ann and I now go into prisons and offer marriage seminars. We show couples how to survive their prison experience, teaching them to rely on the written Word and to believe in each other.

The Lord has also given us a ministry called Life Harvest Missions, which enables us to go into

The Spirit

of God

hit me so hard

I was knocked

off my feet

to my knees.

prisons and hold cookouts with Christian concerts. Ann serves as a community volunteer in a prison where she served part of her time. When an inmate earns a pass, Ann takes the woman out into the community.

The staff brings inmates to our attention on a case-by-case basis. Ann and I then pray together over the women, asking the Lord to direct our steps.

What Satan tried to destroy in our marriage, Jesus was able to heal and to use for His kingdom. If we had not walked through this experience in our lives, we would not have developed a love for people who are incarcerated. We would not have known that kind of love was in us.

In our seminars, Ann often says that the best thing that ever happened to us was her going to prison. It brought me to salvation, and it saved our marriage.

When we speak to inmates, we tell them, "Prison is not the end of your life. It's only the beginning, if you let it be." ❧

With the

help of our

Lord Jesus,

we stayed

together.

T hrough the years, I've often observed how God steers us into that emotional cul-de-sac. He likes to corral us into a corner where the only way out is up. We have nowhere else to turn, and that's when we get serious about praying.

If you're going through a hard time of trouble right now, as so many of us are, don't rail against God for what He has done to bring you to this place.

WAY *but up*

Instead, ask Him how you can learn to be His trusting child and how you can hang on to the desperation that brings about sincere, heartfelt prayer.

"O Lord God, I can't get through one day without You. I can't make it through these next hours without You."

When we become desperate, we cry out, "O Lord, help me!"

And He always does.

DAVID JEREMIAH
FROM A BEND IN THE ROAD

Surrendering to God's Plan

KEN
Danville, Illinois

Our story started back in September of 1999. My wife and I were sick with bronchitis. My health returned to normal, but my wife's health worsened. A month later, in the hospital emergency care, Joan was diagnosed with terminal heart disease and was not expected to live to Christmas. A virus had invaded her heart at some point and had done considerable damage. Needless to say, our lives were immediately changed.

Our three children were devastated by this news. I asked that Joan be transferred to a heart unit that was eighty-five miles away in another state, but the surgery teams said she was too great a risk for surgery. Joan couldn't live a useful life without help, so our family prayed for help and guidance from our Heavenly Father.

On October 30, a surgical team finally agreed to surgery, even though the back of her heart was almost dead. On November 4, she was scheduled to undergo five bypasses and one valve repair.

Our family asked anyone we knew to start a serious prayer vigil for Joan. The request went on the Internet and to four churches located in California, Indiana, and Florida. Numerous Christians around the world were praying for her.

Joan made it through surgery, where she endured seven bypasses and two valve repairs. She then spent eleven weeks in intensive care units, and she lost a leg and had many other problems. Many weekends, I would return home only to receive an urgent call to come back because she had taken a turn for the worse. I felt like I was going crazy from of all of the driving back and forth and spending nights in motels.

One day, I was driving back to Indianapolis and was listening to Tony Evans. Through him, God made me realize that I was helpless, and I turned Joan's life completely over to Him to do as He willed for her.

Joan left the heart center on December 29 and went to a rehab hospital in Indianapolis where she stayed through January 11. She then was transferred closer to home where she went through intense physical therapy. She recovered fairly well and was finally released from the third hospital on February 8, 2000.

God is good. Joan is home doing very well and adjusting to her prosthesis. It will be awhile before she will be completely recovered, but through the grace of God, she will be okay. We know God has a purpose in this for us, and we are ready to do His work however He wants. God has blessed us in many ways through these trials and has given us a longer time together on earth, though all the while we know that to be with Him is far better. ❀

We know

God has

a purpose

in this for us.

The Presence of Christ

VIRGINIA
Columbia, South Carolina

I have experienced a number of bends in the road in my life, including one that slammed me to the very foundations of my being. This turn began with a phone call from the emergency room of our local hospital. The voice on the other end was that of my elderly mother who said that my father was desperately ill.

In my life, my parents had been there to go through crises with me. This time, my parents were a part of the crisis! I ran into the emergency room and saw two people I knew but didn't recognize. Were these really my parents? My big, powerful daddy was so very ill, frail, and utterly helpless. My tiny momma was stricken with grief and terror. This was the man she had loved for over fifty years.

Suddenly, in a matter of minutes, I became my parents' parent. Over the next four years, I also became their money manager, real estate agent, nurse, cook, driver, housekeeper, and protector. I was not a trained caregiver. I had never been *responsible* for anyone else before, and I wasn't really a patient person. How could I possibly handle this and a full-time job?

The first thing I did was pray. "God, please don't let me ever fail them or you," I said. At this point, Jesus began to carry me. I prayed about every decision, every fresh demand, every wrenching pain and agony. And Jesus poured His love, His strength, and His wisdom into me. He did through me what I could NEVER have done on my own.

Night and day, my parents, the two beings other than Jesus whom I loved most in creation, were dying. After my father's death, I had to sell their dream house and eventually retire from a successful career to take care of my mother. In time, my own health began to fail, and ownership of my home hung in the balance. Even the inspiration to write Christian books, a calling I had loved dearly, was gone; the words no longer came.

By the time my mother died, I had nothing left that I owned except my Christian faith and my God who never left me and who made it possible for me to do "all things through Christ who strengthens me" (Phil. 4:13).

God restored my health and home, but more importantly, I realized that faith was enough. When I had nothing but Him, I understood the blessing of leaning on the Lord alone. Thanks be to God! ❀

By the time

my mother

died, I had

nothing

left...

A YOKE
to lighten the burden

Did you ever stop to ask what a yoke is really for?

Is it to be a burden to the animal which wears it?

It is just the opposite:

it is to make its burden light.

Attached to the oxen in any other way

than by a yoke,

the plow would be intolerable;

worked by means of a yoke, it is light.

HENRY DRUMMOND

I will praise You with my whole heart;
> Before the gods I will sing praises to You.
I will worship toward Your holy temple,
> And praise Your name
> For Your lovingkindness and Your truth;
For You have magnified Your word above all Your name.
Though I walk in the midst of trouble,
> You will revive me;
You will stretch out Your hand
Against the wrath of my enemies,
And Your right hand will save me.

PSALM 138: 1–3, 7

In Psalm 138, we find the song of "a man after God's own heart" who had traveled a long journey down the road of spiritual wisdom. He understood many deep truths about his relationship with God—one of which is brought home with clarity and passion here. David came to see that in times of trouble, the most clearly marked path to God is not the way of struggle and desperation.

It is, instead, the path of worship.

David Jeremiah
FROM *A BEND IN THE ROAD*

Out of the Valley

DORIS
Woodruff, South Carolina

I accepted the Lord as my savior as a child. I grew up in a wonderful Christian home with godly parents, and through the years, I really trusted the Lord and lived by faith.

When my dear father had to go to a nursing home, I came to doubt and question everything I'd always lived by. Daddy was such a godly man who loved and served the Lord every day. It was my heart's desire and prayer that the Lord would allow me to take care of my parents in their own home until He called them to their heavenly home. When this didn't happen, I was devastated!

I couldn't go about my normal routine. I just wandered through each day like a zombie. Sleeping was impossible. I felt that if I turned off my lights and went to bed, then I was accepting the fact that my daddy had to go to a nursing home.

> *I battled with God*
>
> *for four months, and it was the*
>
> *coldest, darkest, most desolate*
>
> *time of my life.*

I had always filled my home and car with gospel music and listened to preachers and Bible teachers, but I was so upset that I couldn't listen. I no longer believed the message. I couldn't read my Bible; the words seemed so empty and meaningless.

My precious family was so worried about me. They tried to help, but I felt like God had let us down. I couldn't get beyond that dark despair. Finally, I told my children that if what I had believed all my life was really true, then God would give me a word in some way that would bring me out of my dark valley and give me peace over the situation.

I battled with God for four months, and it was the coldest, darkest, most desolate time of my life. Then one day in February, the meteorologist

predicted a big snow for Friday, my usual shopping day, so I decided to drive into town to run my errands on Wednesday. I flipped on the car radio—something I hadn't done in four months. The station was still set to the gospel station, and a pastor was preaching. Something about his voice got my attention. I began to listen, and the words he spoke were my thoughts and feelings exactly! It was as if he had gotten inside my head. I became so engrossed in what he was saying that I pulled into the nearest parking lot and began taking notes on the back of my grocery list.

Everything he said was exactly what I needed to hear. Then, he said the most amazing statement: "When the time comes and you have to leave a loved one in a hospital or a nursing home and all you can do is hold a withered hand and kiss a wrinkled brow—and when you've done all that you can do—you have to just stand on God's promises. Let it go and give it totally and completely to Him because He is still in control." I knew this was my word straight from my Heavenly Father to me.

I could hardly shop for groceries because I was rejoicing in the realization that God did care for me and had not abandoned Daddy or me. For the first time I could see God's hand in the situation.

I had to drive sixty-five miles to see my daddy, but I believe that God put him just far enough away so that I would have no other choice but to turn his care over to someone else. I was already taking care of my mother, and God knew that I couldn't care for both of them every day in separate places. I also realized that the nursing home was an excellent facility; during Daddy's four-year stay, I never had a complaint about his care.

Through this experience, I became so much closer to the Lord. I learned how to really trust Him completely. His grace changed me! Nine months after Daddy went to the nursing home, my mother went home to heaven. Only a few weeks later, my husband, who hadn't been sick in our thirty-six years of marriage, was diagnosed with a malignant brain tumor and lung and liver cancer. He passed away seven months later. Only a few weeks later, my daddy also passed away.

Within a short time of eighteen months, I lost all three of them in one form or another. Through it all, I can truly say that God's grace is sufficient (2 Cor. 12:9), and His mercies are new every morning—great is His faithfulness! (Lam. 3:21-23). Praise His Holy Name! ❧

In You, O LORD, I put my trust;
Let me never be put to shame.
Deliver me in Your righteousness,
    and cause me to escape;
Incline Your ear to me, and save me.
Be my strong refuge,
To which I may resort continually;
You have given the commandment to save me,
For You are my rock and my fortress.
Deliver me, O my God, out of the hand of the wicked,
Out of the hand of the unrighteous and cruel man.

71 the Lord

For You are my hope, O Lord GOD;
You are my trust from my youth.
By You I have been upheld from birth;
You are He who took me out of my mother's womb.
My praise shall be continually of You.
I have become as a wonder to many,
But You are my strong refuge.
Let my mouth be filled with Your praise
And with Your glory all the day.

PSALM 71:1–8